Urban Wild

Adventure Maps

by
Green Spiral Tours

copyright @2017
updated 2021-Feb
Curator: Angela Wildermuth
Mapmaker: Jessica Hoagland
All rights reserved.
ISBN-13: 978-1542349239

Dedicated to the
Wild Child
in you.

List of Maps

All parks are great for all kids in all weather; here's our list of suggested ages and seasons...

Memorial Park Winter Hike in Brentwood - Bundle up and go on a short hike in January, when the Christmas trees are mulched to make hiking paths. Cross a tiny stream, wander up and down gentle hills, and spy wild birds under the Arch Bridge. Great for that first winter hike.

Deer Creek Park in Maplewood/Webster - Also known as "Rocket Ship Park", this excursion includes a creek walk, boulder scramble, and search for a hidden spring. Put babies in carry packs and expect a two-hour journey for bigger kids.

Tower Grove Park - This park boasts the greatest diversity of trees in America, and the park attracts biodiverse visitors of all kinds. April is a great time to see the baby ducklings and summer is wonderful for a visit to the children's wading pool and farmers market.

Tilles Park Fishing in Ladue - The perfect destination for that first fishing trip. Be like Tom Sawyer and make your own fishing pole. No fishing license required for kids.

Forest Park "Crawdaddy Walk" - America's #1 park and so many things to do! We've mapped a June adventure for catching crayfish with a fish hook made from a paper clip. Missouri is a hotspot for crayfish biodiversity.

Larson Park in Webster Groves - This is a secret creek walk, visit to the 200 year-old "Liberty Tree" and an exploration of a secluded hangout spot. Go in summer with your duck boots.

Shaw Park in Clayton - Home of the Tree Top Adventure Playground, Shaw Park has pop-up water jets in summer, a sensory garden for spring, persimmon picking in autumn and a sledding hill in winter.

Citygarden Downtown - Not originally designed as a children's garden, but nonetheless, perhaps the best children's garden in America. Go when it's hot and play in the water features.

Blackburn Park in Webster Groves - This park has sinkholes to climb *down* into and trees to climb *up* into. The bird sanctuary is a prominent birding site with a bubbling spring and a gentle creek to explore. Go for a treasure hunt in early October when a variety of nuts fall from the trees, and when the persimmons are ripe.

Bellefontaine Cemetery - Surprisingly, cemeteries have long served as children's playgrounds. This is a perfect destination to recover from your Halloween Hangover. Proceed with respect.

Urban Wild

Adventure Maps

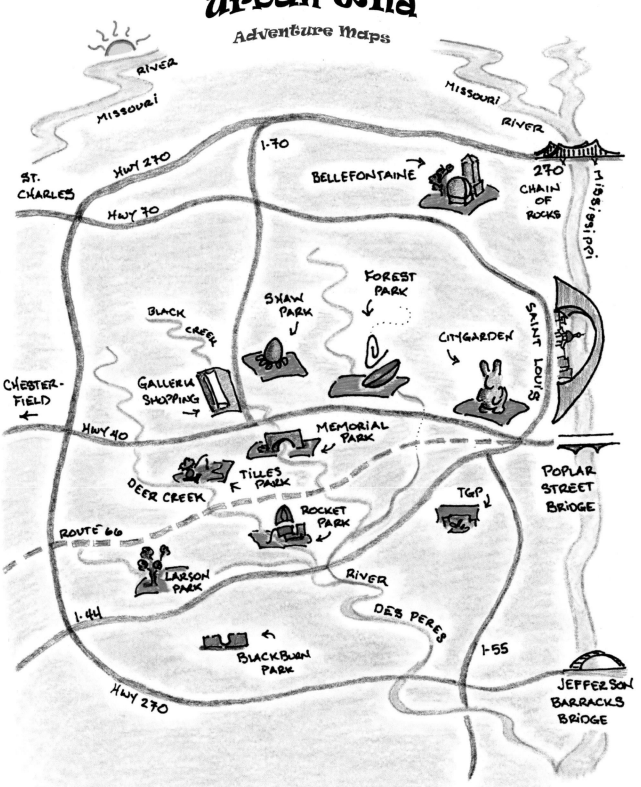

memorial Park

Winter Hike

Winter Hike

Breaking ice with sticks is fun. WCGW?

Memorial Park is a perfect first adventure for building winter resilience and "brown fat" - the kind of fat that keeps you warm in winter. Located in Brentwood, a short winter hike in Memorial Park has scented paths, cardinals, and a destination Arch Bridge at the creek. It's also conveniently located near the Panera fireplace, REI, and the Galleria, where you can recycle personal water while supporting local establishments. The park restrooms are closed in winter.

Winter Tip: buy **rain boots** one size too big, and cut **alpaca foot inserts** to fit, thus creating instant winter boots. Wool socks and foot inserts go a long way towards keeping little toes warm, and small feet will grow into big boots by spring, resulting in a "less but better" solution all around. Bring a **plastic bag** with you, and leave warm liquids in the car for your return.

Start at the **Parking Lot** near the playground. Follow the paved path past the **first bridge** and begin hunting for the **Secret Path**. The Secret Path is marked by an empty **Asphalt Pad** as you approach the **Second Bridge**. Go down the Secret Path towards the **Little Stream**, carefully using the stepping stones to cross the stream. (If the water is too high, cross at the **First Bridge** and follow the stream.)

In January, the paths are freshly mulched and nicely scented with recycled **Christmas Trees**. Explore the paths, climb the bedrock steps, and when given a choice, keep going up and to the left. Don't worry about getting lost, as you can clearly see homes through the honeysuckle. We call this **Honeysuckle Hill**.

Bush honeysuckle is invasive, but **cardinals** love it, so watch for a flash of red, and listen for the sound of "What cheer, cheer, cheer... **What cheer!**" Veer left and downhill until you find your way to the **Arch Bridge**. If the creek is frozen it's fun to break the ice with sticks and rocks. This is **Black Creek**, which flows from behind the **Galleria** to meet the **River Des Peres,** and then on to join the **Mighty Mississippi**. Look for turtles or great blue herons. You might spy some **trash**. If so, use your plastic bag to pick up trash and know the situation gets better every year.

Return by any path to your car and your warm liquids, or make your way to a friendly establishment nearby. Come back in summer to enjoy a completely different experience, by exploring the roller rink, the cool creek and green maze, and the **Sno-Cone** shack in the parking lot. This is a short and sweet adventure of less than one hour, suitable for all ages.

GPS: Memorial Park - 8600 Strassner Road; Brentwood, MO 63144

Panera

Memorial Park

Green Spiral

cardinals

hot chocolate

YMCA

Winter Hike

Southern Sno

"What Cheer!"
"What Cheer!"

great
blue
herons

bundle
up

Black Creek

Honeysuckle
Hill

trash
picker-upper

hiking
project

Arch Bridge

Galleria

REI

wool
socks

Urban Wild Adventures

turtles

plastic bags

rubber
boots

45 minute
adventure

Alpaca
Foot
inserts

8600 Strassner Road
Brentwood 63144

Deer Creek

Rocketship Park

Rocket Ship Park

If kids could vote, Deer Creek Park would be voted the best playground in Saint Louis.

Affectionately known as "**Rocket Ship Park**", the park is maintained by **Maplewood** on one side and **Webster Groves** on the other. **Deer Creek** runs through the middle of the park; it flows south to join the **River Des Peres** (french: "River of our Fathers") and then into the **Mississippi River** (native: "Father of Waters"). A toy boat in Deer Creek could float to the **Gulf of Mexico**.

Due to aging infrastructure, sewers overflow into creeks, especially during big rain storms. Notice the **"No Swimming"** signs, use your judgement, and bring hand **sanitizer**. The **Deer Creek Alliance** is your friend in restoring local creeks, the **Great Rivers Greenway** helps create greenways and bike corridors, and the **Missouri Coalition for the Environment (MCE)**, works with legislators on a policy level to restore the great green world of Saint Louis. Support these worthy non-profits and vote for legislators who will clean up this pretty planet.

Start at the **Playground** and find the **Steep Steps** leading down to the creek, where you can throw rocks, chase minnows, and hunt for "**River Glass**." Listen for the "what-cheer" of **cardinals**, and look around for **mussel** shells on the beach. Walk on the **Stepping Stones** to get to the other side. Fall in. Get wet. Play.

Hike up out of the creek and follow the bike path courtesy of **Great Rivers Greenway.** Notice the **invasive honeysuckle** being replaced by native plants, and be on the lookout for birds, butterflies, **turtles**, **mallards**, ...and bikes! Find the **Rock Walk** and hop from rock to rock as you approach the **Pedestrian Bridge,** which separates Webster Groves from Maplewood. From the bridge, peer deeply into the water to look for **fish,** which appear as dark shadows. Watch for **coal trains** coming from Wyoming to coal fired plants and notice if they are full or empty.

After the bridge, hug the creek and follow the faint path past the giant **Cottonwood Tree**, as well as the **Baseball Diamond**. Hunt for the **Secret Spring** which bubbles up and seeps into **Deer Creek** and invent a magical story when you find it. If it has not rained for a while, the spring will appear as a shallow depression in the ground. Turn right and work your way up the hill using the secret paths until you find the **Boulders;** climb them and follow the ridge trail to **Dotty's Playground.** See if you can find the **geocache** and the "**Ghost Trolley**". **OMGX** is a local outdoor outfitter, located just down the street. Run down the **Steep Hill** used by for **sledding** in winter. Return back across the bridge, use the restrooms to **wash hands,** and get a drink of water or a **sno-cone**. End with snacks or a picnic at **Rocket Ship Park Playground.**

GPS: Deer Creek Park - 3200 Laclede Station Road; Maplewood 63143

Maplewood

OMGX

Webster Groves

Deer Creek

Green Spiral

MCC

secret spring

Honeysuckle

Rocketship Park

Cup of Sno

Sno-cones

cardinals

Dotty's Playground

River Des Peres

Ghost Trolley

sledding

stepping stones

Steep Steps

coal trains

turtles

Pedestrian Bridge

Deer Creek Alliance

Great Rivers Greenway

2 hour adventure

mallards

3200 Laclede Station Rd
Maplewood / Webster 63143

Deer Creek Park
Rocket Ship Park

Tower Grove Park
Tiny Nature Hike

Tiny Nature Hike
TGP

Affectionately known as **TGP**, Tower Grove Park is one of the few remaining Victorian parks in the country, boasting the greatest diversity of trees in America, many of them over 100 years old. This park is biodiverse in food, people, music, habitat and animals.

TGP hosts the **Festival of Nations,** a giant celebration of cultural diversity in August, as well as an annual **Pillow Fight** for grown-ups. Children's music programs are scheduled on Wednesdays at the **Piper Palm House**, while the TGP **Farmers Market** is regularly scheduled for Saturday mornings. We've mapped a tiny nature hike and short family excursion as a diversion while attending one of these many wonderful festivals.

Start at the playground near the **Muckerman Children's Fountain and Wading Pool**. Hold hands and cross the street to the **Flag Circle**; climb the very old **Saucer Magnolias** or **Mulberry Tree,** planted in 1880.

Make your way towards **Ruins Pond,** designed by Henry Shaw using burned stones from the Lindell Hotel, once the largest hotel in America. This pond mimics the great European parks, so bring your toy **Sailboat,** and pretend to be Stuart Little. Look for **Eugene**, the white duck, who is over 10 years old. The **Wood Ducks** are city ducks and are unique to the area.

Look around the **Bald Cypress Trees** for little knees which are only found under very old trees; then find the side-ways growing **Osage Orange Tree** and climb it. Osage orange trees were highly valued by native Americans, who made bows and arrows from its wood. The **Princess Tree** has pretty purple flowers in early April, and the **Fleur de Lis** garden blooms in May. This iris garden was planted in honor of the City's 250th birthday. The iris is the symbol for Saint Louis and legend tells us that the french King Louis knew where to cross the river when returning from war, by the field of yellow irises growing near home.

Wander over to the **Lily Pond** to look for **tadpoles**. Sprinkle drops of water on the lily pads and be amazed at how the water beads up. Look for dragonflies and snapping turtles in summer. Listen for bullfrogs, and look for green frogs as well as leopard frogs in the **Lotus Pond**. In summer, the lotus flowers begin to rise up famously from the muck. Around Mother's Day, find a "sit spot", and settle in to listen for migrating songbirds. This area is a birding hotspot and an **IBA**, an "Important Birding Area" as designated by the Audubon Society.

End by exploring the tiny toddler **Bamboo Adventure** path near the **Ginko Tree,** across from the **Zinc Deer**, an important zinc sculpture in America. OR by bringing a change of clothes and visiting the Wading Pool on a hot summer's day.

GPS: TGP - 4256 Magnolia Avenue; Saint Louis 63110

Queen
of
Flowers

Twangfest

Tower Grove

Green Spiral

tree diversity

sailboat

TGP

Children's Adventure

frogs

Zinc Deer

Lily Pond

Ruins Pond

IBA

Lotus Pond

Eugene
the white duck

Wading Pool

April

dragonflie

tadpoles

Princess Tree

Fleur de Lis

Palm House

2 hour adventure

Osage Orange Tree

4256 Magnolia Avenue
Tower Grove Park 63110

Tower Grove Park
Tiny Nature Hike

MUCKERMAN CHILDREN'S FOUNTAIN AND PLAYGROUND

FARMERS MARKET

TWANGFEST

PILLOW FIGHT

ZINC DEER

START

← SOUTH GATE

CENTER CROSS

NORTH GATE →

CENTER CROSS

SAUCER MAGNOLIA

1880 MULBERRY

SHAKESPEARE

END

GINKO

LILY POND SHELTER

BAMBOO ADVENTURE

TURKISH PAVILION

FROGS

LOTUS POND

POND

PIPER PALMER HOUSE

4256 MAGNOLIA AVE   63110

OFC

GREENHOUSE

G

POND

LILY POND

TAD POLES

1BA

STORYBOOK OAK TREE

FLEUR de LIS

PRINCESS TREE

PLENTY OF PARKING IN THE SHADE

CATTAIL POND

SAILBOAT

EUGENE

RUINS POND

KEY
- ☆ PLAY
- ♥ BE KIND TO ANIMALS
- ♪ LISTEN TO YOU
- ✓ KNOW YOUR FARMER

← EAST GATE

FESTIVAL OF NATIONS

BALD CYPRESS KNEES

SIDEWAYS OSAGE ORANGE TREE TO CLIMB

← ARSENAL →

2020

← GRAND AVE →

Green Spiral

Tilles Park

Fishing Adventure

First Fishing Adventure
Tilles Park Lake

Tom Sawyer went fishing with a simple cane pole, and in the age of DIY YouTube, you can too.

If you don't feel like fishing, then water shoes, a bug net and a magnifying glass can keep kids busy for quite a long time. Tilles Park Lake is stocked with bass, sunfish, catfish and trout, and kids under age 16 do not need a fishing license. Teach kids to stay away from geese, and certainly don't feed them, for geese are mean, and geese bite.

Enter the park from McKnight Road, noting the splash playground on your left. However, veer right towards the main driving loop, and drive until you reach **Skow Shelter** and the **Little Turtle Playground**. Find the **Little Turtle** while waiting for friends, and climb on it.

Start your adventure by heading downhill towards the lake. If it's early October, look for persimmons under the **persimmon tree;** otherwise find the small **climbing trees** near Windegger Shelter and climb them. Try fishing from the **Fishing Dock,** a popular spot.

Watch out for Canadian geese, and see if you can spy the black duck, known as the **Prince of Ducks**. Make your way around the lake, and ignore the **goose poop,** which is really only harmless processed grass. Try your luck at various **fishing spots** while making your way around the lake; say hello to the other fishermen and women.

Find the **willow** trees at the opposite end of the lake, followed by the **"Cyprus Swamp"**, where you can play with **water bugs.** If you brought your net, the water bugs can keep your family busy for quite some time. Look for **Cypress Knees,** which are gnarled roots under very old cypress trees.

Wander around past the **Pines** and pretend you are magical creatures in a **Tiny Woodland**. Walk past the maintenance shed on your right, and make your way back towards Skow Shelter, by **running down** the steep hill and ending up back at the parking lot, using the restroom facilities as necessary.

Visit the **Splash Playground** on the way out. The Splash Playground is the first inclusive playground in Saint Louis and was inspired by a nurse who saw many injuries and wanted to build a safe playground for _all_ kids. It was built by the design firm SWT.

Come back during the holidays to enjoy horse carriage rides and holiday lights, at the famous **Winter Wonderland** display.

GPS: Tilles Lake - 9551 Litzinger Road; Ladue, 63124

Urban Wild

mean Canadian geese

Tilles Park

Green Spiral

goose poop

fishing dock

Fishing Adventure

Tom Sawyer

frogs

turtles

June

Bug Net

catfish

Prince of Ducks

bamboo cane and fishing line

Skow Shelter

carp

tankara

DIY Fishing Pole

persimmons

Oct 1

cypress "swamp"

Little Turtle Playground

2 hour adventure

9551 Litzinger Road
Ladue 63124

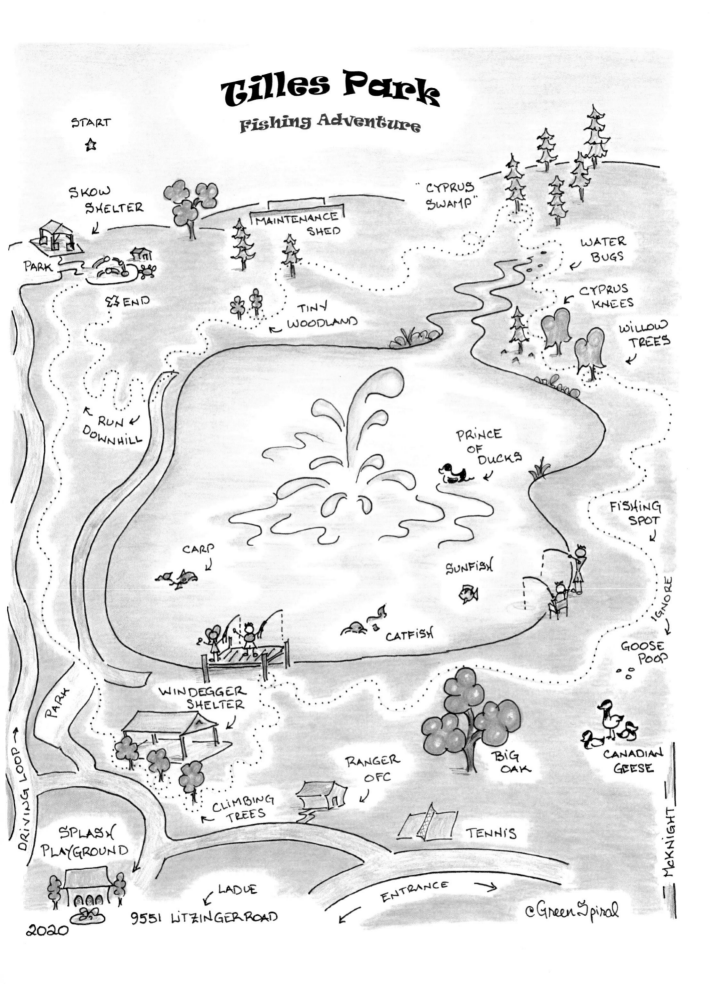

Forest Park

Crawdaddy Adventure

Crawdaddy Walk
Forest Park

Most people know that Forest Park is the crown jewel of Saint Louis city parks, but some folks are surprised to learn that Forest Park is the #1 most beautiful urban park in America.

This is a big park, so we've mapped out a two-hour adventure, moving at a snail's pace with multiple children and a stroller. Thanks to our big beautiful spring-fed rivers, Missouri is a hotspot for crayfish biodiversity -- so gather up a paper clip, a long line of string and a piece of cheese to create a fish-hook for your crayfish adventure. Forest Park is safe, but as in any urban environment, lock your car and always keep valuables out of sight.

Start by meeting your friends on the saucer swing in the **Visitor's Center Playground**. Hunt for the secret pollinator garden nearby, and look for the blueberry bushes growing along the Visitor Center wall. Pick up an official map at the **Visitor's Center** and use the facilities. Walk across **Grand Drive** and follow the path by the **Tennis Complex** while looking for **red clover,** which can be picked to make daisy crowns to wear on your adventure.

Find **Love Locks Bridge.** Here, as in Europe, locks are affixed to the bridge, and the keys are thrown into the river, signifying love that lasts forever. Continue along the path that follows the creek to find the **serviceberry** trees, whose berries ripen just as the ground becomes soft enough to bury the dead. Birds (and some humans) love to eat these berries. A walk through **Cottonwood Corridor** is magical in early June, as cotton puffs float softly through the air like snowflakes; encourage children to chase them. The **Boathouse** has restrooms and refreshments should you be interested now or later.

Follow the creek until you find **Crawdaddy Cove** and **Fairy Falls,** noted as **Lake Riffles** on the official map. The riffles cascade into the "**Waterway**", which is treated municipal water. The original river, the **River Des Peres,** was buried beneath Forest Park in anticipation of the World's Fair; it now functions as an under-gound passageway for wastewater.

Find a place to sit on the obvious rocks and drop your fishing hook and cheese into the water. The **crawdads** (crayfish) will grab ahold of the cheese, and kids can lift the splendid creatures out of the water and into the air, with much excitement and delight. Enjoy your stay while looking for **frogs, egrets, green herons** and **turtles.**

Rest up for the long walk back to the car, and on the way back, peer beneath the **Bridge of Swallows** to watch the swallows come and go. End at the Visitor's Center, where restrooms and drinking fountains can be found, as well as the **Forest Perk Cafe.**

GPS: Forest Park - 5595 Grand Drive; 63112

Visitor's Center

Tennis Complex

Forest Park

biodiversity

Green Spiral

waterway

Boathouse

Crawdaddy Walk

frogs

Love Locks Bridge

River Des Peres

turtles

home-made crawdad fish-hook

picnic

paperclip, string & cheese

Fairy Falls

June

egrets

crayfish

service berries

Forest Park

Bridge of Swallows

2 hour adventure

"Cottonwood Corridor"

5595 Grand Drive
Forest Park, 63112

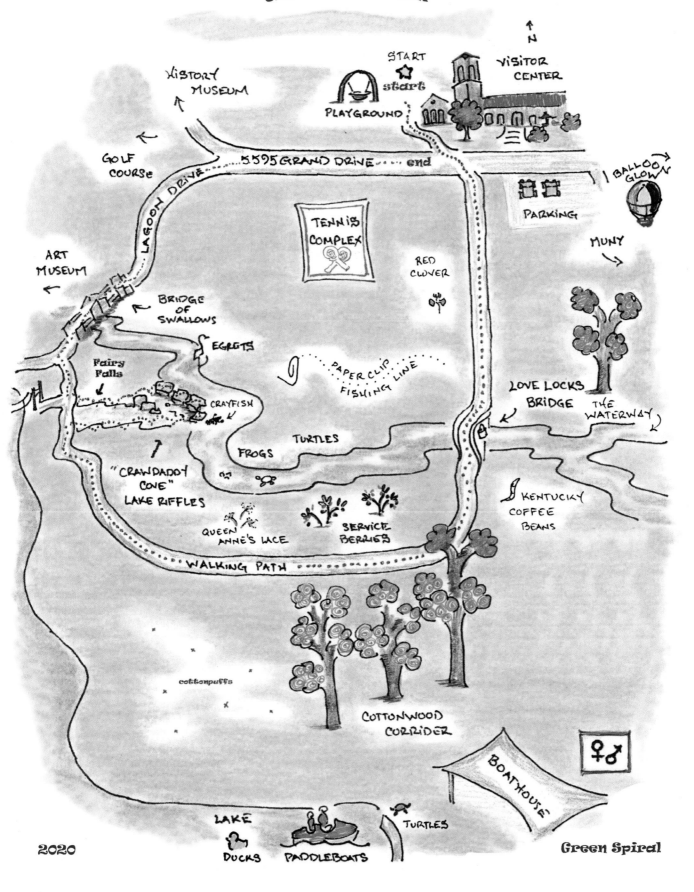

Forest Park
Crawdaddy Walk

Larson Park

Creek Walk

Secret Creek Walk
Larson Park

Larson Park is one of the best nature places for kids, and it remains largely undiscovered.

We've mapped out a two-hour "Secret Creek Walk"; so put kids in rain boots, and go when it's fairly warm. Bring hand sanitizer, knowing that sewers overflow into creeks from time to time. Early explorers drank whisky, hard cider or beer, as opposed to river water, which made people sick due to e.coli (animal poop).

Start at the **playground** near the **pavilion,** walk past the **Bald Cypress** tree and then over the **First Bridge**. As you approach the **Second Bridge**, drop down into the creek, instead of crossing the bridge. Walk along the smooth flat bedrock, looking for **potholes**, and wonder how long the pebbles had to swirl to make the little potholes. Travel as far as you like, then turn around and come back. While exploring the creek, think about ways to slow down water, which rushes ever faster in modern life, scouring creeks down to the bedrock and washing away habitat for tiny little creatures.

Follow the creek and look for the **Sideways Sycamore Tree;** climb it while you contemplate the beauty of **Shady Grove Creek**. Rest on the **bench** chopped out of a tree trunk. Continue to follow the creek, gently downhill, until you find the giant **Liberty Tree**. Read the plaque and give a salute to this 200 year old tree.

Continue downhill to enter the woodland, and walk until you find the **Hangout Spot** and **Super Steep Hill** to climb. Climb up and down the hill, and get dirty. Notice the **Wall**, then turn around to follow the path back along the creek. There are multiple ways to cross back over the creek, depending on your balance and sense of adventure. Enjoy the creek, look for fossils, skip rocks and float little leaf boats down to the Gulf of Mexico. When you pop up out of the creek on the other side, you will follow the fence past the **Baseball Diamond** and thus back to your starting point.

Hop on rocks in the **Rain Garden** near the restroom. Know that rain gardens are designed to help slow down water. Linger a few moments by hanging on the **Swing Tree,** to burn off any remaining energy before getting back into the car and returning home.

GPS: Larson Park - 520 W. Kirkham; Webster Groves 63119

Urban Wild

adventure

Larson Park

Green Spiral

bedrock

undiscovered

Swing Tree

Secret Creek Walk

frogs

Hang out Spot

July

turtles

fossils

Shady Grove Creek

Super Steep Hill

Second Bridge

rain boots

potholes

Hop on rocks

Skip Rocks

hand sanitizer

2 hour adventure

sideways sycamore

520 W. Kirkham
Webster Groves 63119

LARSON PARK
Creek Walk

SWING TREE

FOSSILS

"POTHOLES"

PARKING

START

FIREPIT

RAIN GARDEN

SIDEWAYS SYCAMORE TO CLIMB

BENCH

LIBERTY TREE

SHADY GROVE CREEK

SUPER STEEP HILL TO CLIMB

TEEN HANG OUT

WALL

LOWER PARKING

N

520 W. Kirkham; Webster Groves 63119

2020

Green Spiral

Shaw Park

Family Adventures

Family Adventure Map
Shaw Park

Shaw Park is the crown jewel of Clayton Parks, and a destination park for any season, so we've mapped a short adventure that starts in the Sensory Garden and ventures forth from there.

Beware the Google address for Shaw Park, and set your GPS for the parking lot near the Clayton High School at **2 Mark Twain Circle**, 63105. Find your way to the **Sensory Garden**.

Begin at the ceramic **Egg**, made by notable ceramic artist Carol Fleming. The egg symbolizes hope, so give it a hug and a pat, and maybe even a kiss. The **Sensory Garden** was one of the first of its kind in Saint Louis and was made to touch and feel, so wander about, pinching plants and sniffing things.

Look for the cement bird baths on the ground, cast from leaves of "**elephant ears**", a giant tropical plant. Enjoy the Sensory Garden and find small **hiding places**. In fall, spy the apples growing along the espalier wires in fall. **Espalier** is a french word that describes the way plants are trained to grow along a wall or wire.

After exploring the Sensory Garden, travel through the **living tunnel** and ring the wind chimes. Proceed to the waterfall and notice the "**Do Not Climb**" sign, installed shortly after the first Green Spiral adventure. The waterfall looks just like an adventure playground!

On your way to or from the **Adventure Playground**, don't miss climbing on "**One of Us on a Tricycle**". Kids are allowed to climb into the face of this sculpture, but beware, the sculpture is very hot in summer and very slippery when wet. It's good for kids to take calculated risks.

When you're ready to go wandering, head for the clever **geocache** hidden on a bench near the swimming pool. On your way, find a "sit spot" at the **Nature Area** and listen to the hum of insects, which are attracted by the native plants and grasses. Find the loose rocks at the **Rock Place** and stack them up to make sculptures, or "cairns". In August, look for **monarch** butterflies in the Nature area, and say "hola" or "adios" as they pass through on their way to Mexico. Enjoy the **water features** and float little leaves down the **waterfalls**.

Look for nesting **hawks** and enjoy the **bats** which go hunting over the baseball fields at night. Know that the bats are eating mosquitos and they will not harm you. If you play ball in early October, hunt for **persimmon trees**. You will know them by their lego-like bark, and by the persimmons that fall to the ground under the trees. On your way back to the car, find the giant **Twin Sister Cottonwood** tree and look for the burned bark, where a car crashed and caught fire, many years ago.

GPS: Shaw Park - 2 Mark Twain Circle; Clayton, 63105

Urban Wild

Clayton

Shaw Park

Green Spiral

geocache

pop-up jets

Exercise Loop

Adventure Playground

bats

Waterfall

hawks

Summer

inclusive

Sensory Garden

One of Us on a Tricycle

Pat the Egg

monarchs

dragonflies

sledding

Nature Area

Rock Sculptures

1 hour adventure

Persimmons Oct 1

2 Mark Twain Circle
Clayton 63105

Shaw Park
Adventure Map

Citygarden

Children's Water Play

Citygarden for Kids

Citygarden was not originally designed as a children's garden, but when it first opened, and kids jumped into the water, Citygarden hired lifeguards and said, "Come on in!"

This is a **"Free to Play"** destination that is sculpture park, native garden, water playground and public commons, all mixed together into one wonderful new thing. It's one of America's great public spaces, and a model of sustainable practices. Plus it's free! Go when it's hot, and play in the water features. Take teenagers at night and enjoy the ambience and lighting.

Park near the **Porta Potty** on 10th Street, or **metro** to the 8th & Pine station. Start with a family photo at the **Two White Rabbits** who are loved so much, they must be repainted each year. Notice the **Door of Return** on your way to the **Pop-Up Jets**. The Door of Return invokes the feeling of a seed splitting open -- it's also a busy pokemon gym. Watch while kids play in the pop-up jets, and look for the sleeping cat in the **Voyage** sculpture boat. Find the **musical** pads hidden behind the bushes, and play 'Twinkle, Twinkle' with your feet. Look for the giant **Pinocchio** sculpture on your way to the **Fire and Ice Cream Truck** or other food trucks.

The **Security Officers** are very friendly, and will give your dog a treat; think up a question to ask them. Pick up an official **map,** and read about the sculptures, the architecture, the plants and the water features. Take a family photo at the waterfall, which represents Missouri river bluffs. The best time to visit the Citygarden is during the **Pink Flamingo Party** in fall, when kids race their very own **Pink Rubber Ducky** over the waterfall.

Make your way to the giant head and **Tilted Disk**, and climb around inside, or have big kids help each other climb on top. Make a big noise by throwing a soccer or tennis ball around inside. Visit **Kaldis** on **Mother's Day**, and search for the **peonies** blooming behind the serpentine wall. Peonies always have ants. Climb on the **Aesop's Fables** sculpture, and know the one thing you're not allowed to do is climb across the top beam of this giant red sculpture.

Walk past the **Video Wall,** and notice how kids ignore it in favor of nature. Climb the mound to check out the **Zenit** sculpture. Make your way back to your car, and say goodbye to digital walkers **Bruce & Sara**. Recycle your map along the way.

GPS: Citygarden - 801 Market Street; Saint Louis, 63101

sculpture garden

Citygarden

Green Spiral

waterfall

Gateway Foundation

Audio Tour

Free to Play!

Pink Rubber
Ducky Races

peonies
bloom

spray
plaza

Please Touch

Door of
No Return

Musical Pads

Aesop's
Fables

bring
your dog

White Rabbits

Pinocchio

Bruce
&
Sarah

Awards

zenit

lifeguards

children's garden

Mother's Day adventure

Kaldi's
Coffee

801 Market Street
Downtown STL; 63101

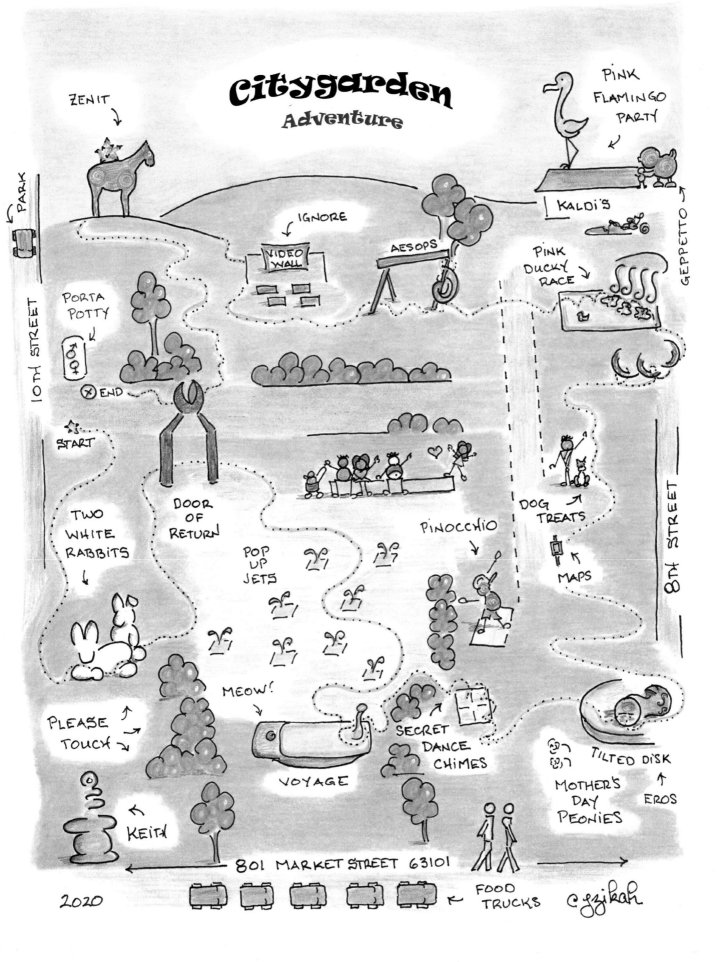

Blackburn Park

Sinkholes and Sanctuariees

Fall Treasure Hunt
Blackburn Park

In fall, Blackburn Park is a treasure hunt for persimmons, pinecones and nuts inside sinkholes. In spring it's a visit to a beautiful hidden creek inside a bird sanctuary.

This map depicts a one hour journey into the sinkholes of Blackburn Park in search of nature's treasures. If you decide to extend your adventures into the bird sanctuary, consider this a two-hour adventure. The bird sanctuary map is still in progress...

Start at the **Toddler Playground**, and make your way to the big sinkhole across the path. We've named this **Big Boy Sinkhole**. Drop in and out of Big Boy, then make your way to **Sassy Sinkhole**, named for the Sassafras trees located at the edges. Identify sassafras trees by their leaves that are shaped like mittens. Root beer comes from sassafras; bite into a leaf and see how it tastes. Look for a climbing tree, and climb it. Climb out of Sassy and go down into nearby **Hickory Hole**, named for its Shagbark Hickory Tree. Look around on the ground for hickory nuts.

Finish exploring Hickory Hole, and wander along the back fence through **Pinecone Alley**. Collect pine cones and notice the differences between them. Continue along the fence, passing the **Kentucky Coffee Trees**, and pick up the pods, once used as a coffee substitute. Find the Catalpa Tree, and play with the long cigar-shaped seeds called **Lady Cigars**. If you don't like lady cigars, use them for a tiny sword fight.

Decide whether or not to drop into the **Bird Sanctuary**. If yes, take any path downhill and find the limestone ledge, bubbling spring and creek. Follow the creek and use the stepping stones to cross over the tiny creek several times. Play with sticks in the mud or make tiny leaf boats and float them on the water. Follow the creek to where it ends, then turn around and find your way back uphill, and out of the bird sanctuary. Research the bird sanctuary before you go, and learn all about birder **Phoebe Snetsinger**.

Exit the bird sanctuary by the river birches, and proceed towards the parking lot past the tennis court, looking for two tall skinny **Persimmon Trees**. You will know them by the bark that looks like lego pieces and by the persimmons that fall on the ground in very early October. Taste a few ripe persimmons after picking them up off the ground and dusting them off. Persimmons will make you thirsty, so make your way past the pavilion to visit the **drinking fountain**. End where you started at the **Toddler Playground.**

GPS: Blackburn Park - 509 Edgar Road; Webster Groves, 63119

Webster Groves

Blackburn Park

Green Spiral

Persimmons

Birds

Sassafras
Trees

Sink Holes

Shagbark
Hickory Tree

Bubbling Spring

Phoebe Snetsinger

Toddler
Playground

"Lady Cigars"

Pinecone
Alley

Fall Treasures

Bird Sanctuary

One Hour
Treasure Hunt

Kentucky
Coffee
Beans

Urban Wild

509 Edgar Road
Webster Groves
63119

Blackburn Park
fall treasure hunt

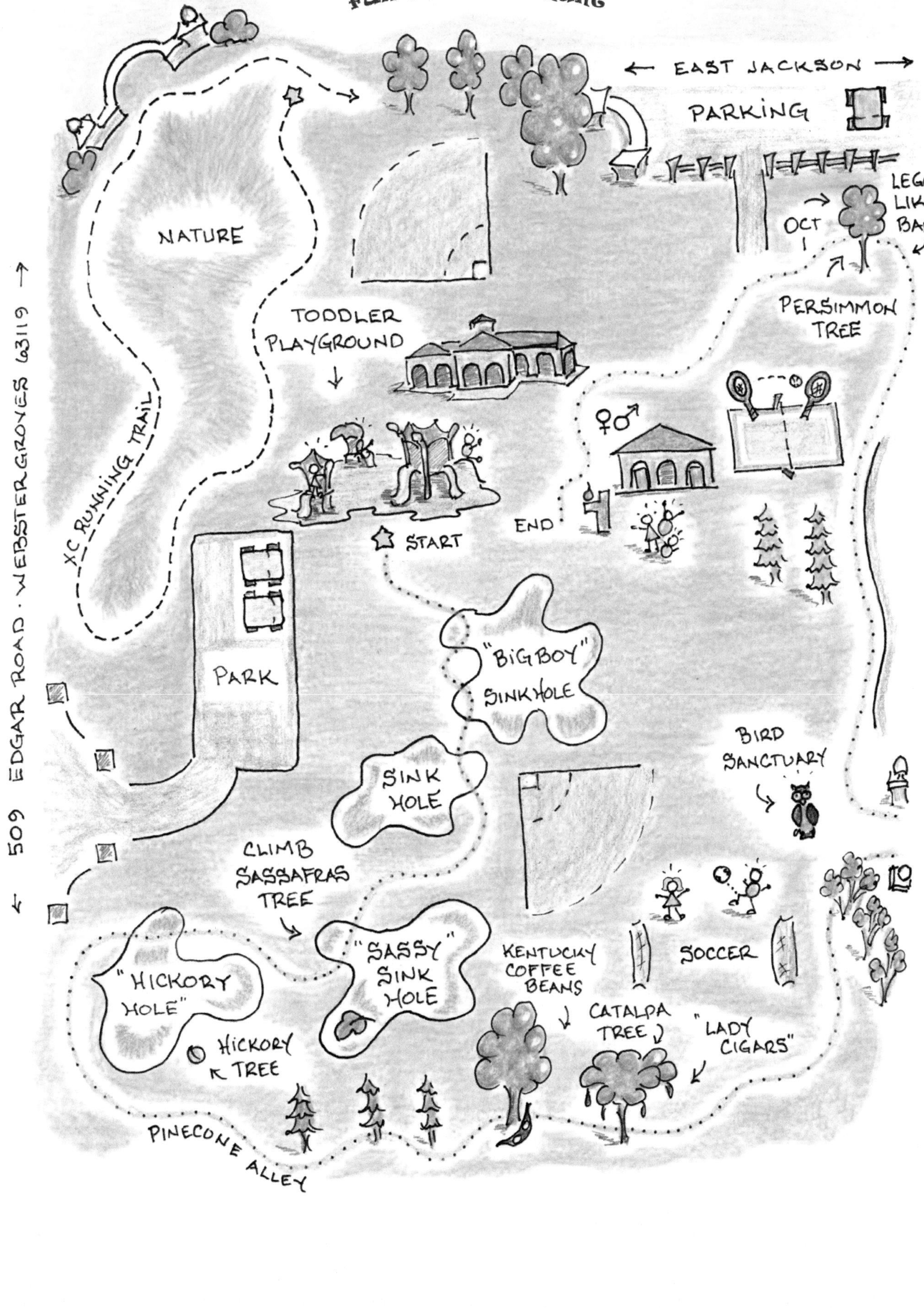

509 EDGAR ROAD · WEBSTER GROVES 63119 →

← EAST JACKSON →

PARKING

NATURE

OCT 1

LEGO LIKE BARK

PERSIMMON TREE

TODDLER PLAYGROUND

XC RUNNING TRAIL

START

END

PARK

"BIG BOY" SINKHOLE

BIRD SANCTUARY

SINK HOLE

CLIMB SASSAFRAS TREE

"HICKORY HOLE"

Hickory Tree

"SASSY" SINK HOLE

KENTUCKY COFFEE BEANS

CATALPA TREE

SOCCER

"LADY CIGARS"

PINECONE ALLEY

Bellefontaine

Halloween Hangover

Halloween Hangover

Surprisingly, cemeteries were our first playgrounds, as families once visited their dearly departed with picnics on Sundays. Many people are also surprised to discover that **Bellefontaine Cemetery** is an arboretum and a nature preserve. This is a lovely two hour adventure for kids and a nice first driving adventure for teens. The day after Halloween is a particularly nice time to go.

Bellefontaine has french roots, so you can pronounce it either the french way, "Belle-fon-TANE" or the common way: "Belle-FOUNTAIN". Both are correct. Note that approaching by Shreve Avenue is more pleasant than approaching by Kingshighway.

Enter the **Main Gate**, park in the obvious spot and buzz into the **Main Office** to pick up an Arboretum map, a Cemetery map and a bottle of water. Cross over to buzz into the charming Gate House to use the **restrooms** before you begin your explorations.

Consult your cemetery map and head for the *Columbarium* in **Wildwood Valley**. The **Columbarium** is a bubbling sanctuary where cremated remains are interred. Kids say that when a bubble comes up, "an angel's wish comes true". Proceed with respect, and enjoy the water gardens by quietly hopping on rocks all the way down to **Cascade Lake**.

Head back into the car and find tree #34 on your Arboretum map. This is a **Champion American Elm**. See if you can hold hands and make a ring around the trunk of this great tree. Look for little holes where thousands of gallons of pesticides are injected each year to protect this fragile species. Wander up the hill to the **Scenic Overlook** to see if you can spy the **Mississippi River**, visible over rows and rows of warehouses.

Next, use your official map for a long and winding driving tour, making sure to pass the **Wainwright Tomb** (#29) as well as the **Beer Baron** tomb (#13). Pay attention to the oldest part of the cemetery, the **Hempstead Cemetery** (#17) and notice **Evergreen Meadows**, where you can get a green burial. Get out of the car to offer a penny to explorer **William Clark** (#16). At the end of your trip, take a right to leave the white line and find the **Garden of Angels**, where babies are buried. Or, continue off the beaten track to find **Mother Mulberry** (#48), a nice place for a quiet picnic.

Bellefontaine Cemetery is quite large and historically significant; you will want to return many times, possibly to see the daffodils in March or to attend the **Beer Baron Tour** in October. Leave a donation as so inspired before you depart.

GPS: 4947 W. Florissant; Saint Louis, 63115

Wainwrght Tomb #29

green burials

Green Spiral

Bellefontaine

Columbarium

Tree #34

Captain Clark

Flameless Cremation

Nature Preserve

Halloween Hangover

Cascade Lake

scenic overlook

Wildwood Valley Gardens

Main Gate

Sanctuary

Beer Baron Tour

Garden of Angels

white line

foxes

Maps

Arboretum

tulips

Mother Mulberry Tree #48

Hempstead Cemetery #17

2 hour adventure

Adolphus Busch Tomb #13

4947 W. Florrissant STL 63115

Bellefontaine
Cemetery & Arboretum

17 HEMPSTEAD

EVERGREEN MEADOW

34 CHAMPION AMERICAN ELM

WILLIAM CLARK FAMILY PLOT

16

13 BEER BARON

29 WAIN WRIGHT TOMB

48 MOTHER MULBERRY

COLUMBARIUM

CYPRESS LAKE

END

GARDEN OF ANGELS

PARK

START

MAIN OFFICE

PICK UP MAPS

CASCADE LAKE

GATE HOUSE

WILDWOOD VALLEY GARDENS

4947 W. FLORISSANT 63115

2020

@zikah

Urban Wild Adventures

This is Angela Wildermuth, an Urban Wild Nature Guide with a gift and a passion for sharing nature with children. Angela's last name means "wild spirit".

In this series you can follow Angela off-the-beaten track into popular Saint Louis parks to explore sinkholes, springs, creeks, and other hidden adventures.

These maps are based on real adventures with real families, in sunshine, rain, sleet and snow -- and what's in them can't be found on the internet. We've done our best to bring forth what will surprise and delight you, and what will encourage you to venture forth on your own grand adventures.

Children learn through their bodies and absorb most of their love of nature before age six. So it's important to get kids outside and "into the wild" from a young age. We think you'll enjoy these learning adventures, which have been carefully curated by Angela and field tested by Green Spiral families.

Bring family and friends with you when you go, to share both the magic and the misadventures, and remember that misadventures make children more resilient. If you can manage to rally up a group, it will turn your adventure into a "super learning" experience.

We hope these maps will inspire you to explore the urban wild places around you, and fall ever more in love with your place on the planet.

To book a nature trip with Angela,
Find her on the Urban Wild Facebook Page.

Green Spiral Tours

My name is Jessica Hoagland and I started Green Spiral Tours in 2008 to connect families with nature and people to their planet. Green Spiral Tours specializes in "one of a kind" field trips, usually with a green or eco-literacy theme.

Saint Louis is a magical place for children and the range of family adventures in this great city is truly amazing. These maps represent the best urban wild adventures for young families, and we've created them so that you can create your own adventures, at your own pace, and on your own time.

I am the mapmaker, and Angela is the curator.

It's exciting to watch local parks go native with an eye towards children. Native plants attract wildlife, and wild creatures attract children back into the garden. Going unplugged is good for you, and it's important to tune into nature from a very young age.

These are not GPS maps, which your gadget with the blue dot can do better. They are adventure maps designed to launch you on your own adventures and help you fall ever more in love with your place on the planet.

It turns out, if you love your planet, your planet will love you back!

We're curious to know about your family adventures, and we'd love to publish the best of them. Please forward children's art and funny family adventure stories to the email below for consideration.

GreenSpiralTours@gmail.com
www.GreenSpiralTours.com

Made in the USA
Monee, IL
16 June 2022